5U

1

X

D1017087

12/13

CLEANING
Hints & Tips

CLEANING

Hints & Tips

Cindy Harris

RYLAND
PETERS
& SMALL
LONDON NEW YORK

First published in the United States
in 2005 by Ryland Peters & Small, Inc.
519 Broadway, 5th Floor
New York, NY 10012
www.rylandpeters.com
10 9 8 7 6 5 4 3 2
Text © copyright Cindy Harris 2005

Design and photographs © copyright Ryland
Peters & Small 2005

The text in this book has previously been published
by Ryland Peters & Small, Inc. in *Keeping House* by
Cindy Harris.

Library of Congress Cataloging-in-Publication Data

Harris, Cindy, 1947-
  Cleaning hints & tips / Cindy Harris.
    p. cm.
  Includes index.
  ISBN 1-84172-849-7
1. House cleaning. I. Title.
  TX324.H3555 2005
  648'.5--dc22   2004016253

Printed in China

DESIGNER Saskia Janssen
EDITOR Sharon Cochrane
PICTURE RESEARCHER Emily Westlake
PRODUCTION Sheila Smith
ART DIRECTOR Gabriella Le Grazie
PUBLISHING DIRECTOR Alison Starling

CONTENTS

INTRODUCTION

Your home should be a place in which you can relax, feel comfortable, and restore yourself from the stresses and strains of the day. Only by keeping your home in tiptop condition can it become a refuge for you and your family. A neglected home becomes a chaotic and unhappy place, whereas a home that is well kept will not only be a pleasure to come back to, but it will improve your mental wellbeing—if your home is in order, the rest of your life will feel manageable.

Think of shiny tubs and basins, sparkling faucets, and a grime-free oven. Clean windows and scrubbed floors. You really don't have to be superhuman to get your home looking this good. All you need are the tools, the know-how, and a routine that works for you and your family. This book will give you all these things, including a beautifully clean home that will sparkle.

GETTING YOUR HOME

IN ORDER

SIMPLE HOME MANAGEMENT

Your home is your castle, and you are the master of this domain. This thought may be overwhelming, but it needn't be. Just follow a few simple rules for creating an orderly routine that will turn housekeeping into an art form. Establishing priorities and setting realistic goals in your daily schedule are essential. Clean the rooms in which you spend the most time and those where cleanliness is a priority. You can let everything else go, at least for a while. Write down what needs to be done that day, do it, then check it off.

HOUSEKEEPING: A STATE OF MIND

If you can change the way you think around the home, you will save yourself a lot of time and effort keeping your house clean and neat. Adopt the key attitudes below, and you and your home will instantly benefit.

Live neat Make this your new mantra. Being tidy is a state of mind that will become a lifestyle! Do not let things accumulate on tables, countertops, or in the sink, but have everything back in its proper place as you go along. Put soiled clothes in the hamper and hang up all clothes as soon as you've taken them off (if they are still clean). Avoid the urge to drop things or put things down where they don't belong, and don't let your family do it either. There will be no one to pick them up but you, and by leaving them, you create a mountain of work for yourself.

Do it now, not later Put away newspapers, magazines, and similar items as you go along. Don't leave it for later in the day because it will always look worse then. Later can easily become tomorrow, or the next day, and then next week—resulting in a pile of mess and chaos.

Think ahead A useful tip is to keep a list of essential supplies that you need to buy, which can be added to when you see that you've run out—or preferably, before you run out—of them. There's nothing worse than running out of a vital item at 10:00 at night!

GETTING INTO A ROUTINE

In order to keep your housework under control, you need to create a system that makes sense for you, your home, and the people you live with. The demands of a large house will not be the same as those of a studio apartment; and the home of a full-time working couple will not need the same upkeep as a house occupied by a family with two children and a dog. You may have hours to spend each day on keeping your home clean and neat, or you may only have a few hours during your busy working week. Whatever your lifestyle, however, the housework basics are the same.

ESSENTIAL DAILY TASKS

If you don't have time to do the more arduous jobs around the home, simplify your routine as much as possible by doing only the essential daily tasks. These entail keeping the bathroom(s), bedroom(s), and kitchen cleaned.

Bathroom(s) Clean surfaces and faucets with a cloth soaked in a disinfectant bathroom cleaner or multisurface spray. To avoid the buildup of scum, wipe down the shower cubicle or bathtub with a sponge or cloth after each use. Spraying shower cubicles with a special shower spray will prevent the buildup of mineral deposits. A scummy bathtub or shower is not inviting to use. Hang wet towels to dry, but if they are sopping wet, change them. Your facecloth may need to be changed daily for hygienic purposes.

Bedroom(s) Make the beds first thing in the morning, but try to air them for a while first. Ventilate the bedrooms for at least half an hour every day, if you can.

Kitchen Keep the kitchen clean, dishes washed, and pantry well stocked at all times. Clean up pots and pans as you go along or stack them in the dishwasher. Even if you haven't got a full load, run a rinse cycle to prevent food from crusting over, or rinse them under the faucet. Put out clean dishtowels and cleaning utensils daily.

Floors Clean the floors in high-use areas, like the kitchen and entryway, especially if you have young children or pets. Sweep, damp mop, or vacuum as necessary.

Foods Always keep some fresh vegetables, salad-makings, and fruit available for a quick, healthy meal, whenever time is short.

General cleaning Although maid service can be expensive, if you can't afford household help once a week, try to arrange to share a domestic with a friend. Choose the most arduous tasks for the professional to do, such as cleaning windows.

Laundry Try to do a little bit of laundry, whether it's washing, drying, or ironing, twice a week, before it becomes an overwhelming chore. If cost-efficiency is your top priority, wait until you have a full load before doing the washing.

Trash cans Empty trash and garbage containers every day, as a matter of hygiene.

WEEKLY TASKS

Each of these jobs should be tackled at least once a week, some of them more often. Try to establish a weekly routine for these chores, so you have a clear idea of what needs to be done on which day.

• Change bed linens.

• Toss pillows into a hot dryer for 15 minutes to freshen and eliminate dust mites.

• Change bath towels twice a week.

• Vacuum carpets and rugs twice a week; floors, upholstered furniture, and lampshades weekly.

• Wash all hard-surface floors, such as stone, marble, and slate, using a commercial floor cleaner.

• Dust all surfaces and objects that can be dusted, including pictures (don't forget the tops), mirrors, light fixtures, and light bulbs.

• Wipe all fingerprints or smears from doorknobs, woodwork, telephones, and computer keyboards. Use a soft cloth and antibacterial spray.

• Wash off the entire bathroom: toilet, sink, wall tiles, toothbrush holders, fixtures, cabinets, and floor.

• Clean the entire kitchen: clean the refrigerator; wipe the stove (oven and burners) and other appliances inside and out; clean sinks, counter- and tabletops; wash backsplashes; scrub the floor.

- Clean the oven linings if they are washable—catalytic linings shouldn't be scrubbed. You may need to clean the interior more often, depending on usage.
- Wash out and sanitize garbage cans. Germs can, and do, accumulate there.
- Do food shopping once a week. If you keep an up-to-date market list of what you need for the next meals, and what items you have run out of, this should be easy. Attach your list to a pin board in the kitchen and write down what you need to buy when you think of it. Mark one day of the week as your market day. Pick up extra items on interim marketing days: for instance, a certain day for the fish market, and another for your farmers' market (if you have one), and neighborhood store for forgotten items.
- Miscellaneous jobs: for example, cleaning out a utility drawer, going through old cosmetics, throwing out medicines that have expired, and so on.

MONTHLY TASKS

Some of these jobs will need to be handled once a month, others slightly less frequently.

- Wash mirrors and glass panels at least once a month.
- Launder all bed linens, including mattress covers, blankets, pillow covers, quilts, and comforters at least once every three months.
- Turn most frequently used mattresses every four to six months—flip from bottom to top as well as from side to side. You will need help with this.
- Vacuum the mattresses when you flip them.
- Launder pillows according to the directions on the tags.
- Clean range-top hood every two to four months.
- Wax or condition floors every three to six months, depending on use.
- Go through drawers, cabinets, and closets frequently to toss out what you no longer use and to clean out anything that's become sticky. Add moth cakes to clothes drawers and closets. Get into the habit of tackling one drawer or cabinet a week in rotation, particularly in the kitchen and bathroom, until they are all done.
- Clean and polish metal household items at least every three to six months. Be careful to use the appropriate product for different metals: silver polish should not be used on brass, pewter, and so on.

ANNUAL TASKS
These tasks will need to be dealt with once every six to twelve months, depending on usage.

• Clean chandeliers, lamps, and any other light fixtures once a year, or more often if they are unusually dusty.

• Clean all wall surfaces, such as paneling and plaster, at least twice a year. You will probably need to remove finger smudges from walls more frequently than this. This can be done using a rag moistened with a solution made from one-quarter cup ammonia and one cup water.

• Clean your storage areas once a year. Invest in good metal filing cabinets to store archival files and mementos. Throw out old boxes that won't be used.

• Move all large appliances, such as the stove and refrigerator, and vacuum and damp-mop the area beneath and behind them at least once a year.

• Shampoo upholstery and carpeting (or call in a professional service) every one to two years, depending on the area's usage. A carpeted bathroom or dining room will need shampooing at least once a year.

• Oil or condition baseboards every six to twelve months.

• Wash windows and screens a minimum of twice a year.

• Launder or dryclean window treatments, such as drapes and Roman shades, every year.

- Go through your collection of books, CDs, videos, and DVDs and dispose of what you no longer want; your public library will have a use for them and can give you a tax-deductible receipt. Keep ahead of this task by doing it once a year.
- Go through your clothes; if you haven't worn an item in the last two years, it's time for it to go. If you don't make room for the new, nothing new will come into your life. And if it does, you won't have a place for it!

CLEANING
BASICS

GETTING THE JOB DONE

In order to keep your home clean and sparkling, you need to have some basic cleaning tools and products. You will also need to know how to carry out basic techniques, such as dusting and mopping, to keep your house in tiptop condition. Before you start, make sure you have all the cleaning materials you need close by.

Cleaning Products

- Use cleaning products only on the surfaces and in the manner recommended on the label.
- Don't use a harsh cleaner when a mild all-purpose product will do the job.
- When mixing solutions, pour in the water before the cleanser so you don't risk splashing the undiluted product on surrounding surfaces.
- A concentrated cleanser is more effective diluted than straight out of the bottle.
- Always test a new product on a small area before using it.
- To save time, put together a basic cleaning kit composed of products you need to clean the kitchen and the rest of the house. Keep this kit in a caddy organizer in an easy-to-access place, such as under the kitchen counter. Every home is different, so go from room to room in your own home, making a list of all the cleaning products you are going to need. It's a good idea to keep a discreet cleaning kit in areas of high use, such as the kitchen, the bathroom, and the laundry.

Basic Cleaning Kit

- Absorbent paper towels
- All-purpose household cleanser
- Ammonia
- Antimildew tile and tub cleanser
- Baking soda
- Caddy organizer, with a handle
- Dishwashing liquid
- Disinfectant cleanser
- Furniture polish
- Isopropyl or rubbing alcohol
- Large and small nylon brushes
- Lint-free cotton cloths
- Microfiber cloth
- Non-chlorine bleach
- Nylon scrubbing pad
- Sponge
- Squeegee
- White vinegar
- Window cleaner

HOMEMADE CLEANERS

In addition to knowing which cleaning products you need for each room and surface in your home, it's a good idea to be able to create your own cleaning solutions from common household ingredients. The following all-purpose disinfectant cleansers are generally safe to use on most surfaces.

Mild All-purpose Cleanser

• Mix one-quarter cup baking soda with one quart warm water.
• Wipe the surface or structure, then rinse.

Concentrated All-purpose Cleanser

Do not use these solutions on aluminum, marble, crystal, or porcelain.
• Add one tablespoon each of ammonia and liquid laundry detergent to one pint warm water, and stir well.
• Alternatively, add a half cup washing soda to one gallon warm water.

Semi-abrasive Cleanser

This will remove difficult stains on various surfaces in your home and can be used as an alternative to commercial scouring powders.
• Make a thick paste with baking soda and water. Apply to the surface with a sponge or a cloth.

Window Cleaner

• Fill a spray bottle nearly to the top with half water and half rubbing alcohol. Top with ammonia and shake lightly.

• Spray on the window, then wipe with a dry, lint-free cloth.

Detergent Solution

This solution is good for cleaning grease or water-soluble stains on most surfaces.

• Mix one teaspoon clear dishwashing liquid or detergent powder (containing no bleaches or strong alkalis) with one cup warm water.

• Dampen a white rag in this solution and carefully rub out the stain. Rinse well.

Ammonia Solution

This is effective in cleaning stubborn floor stains, as well as kitchen appliances and painted wall surfaces. Caution should be used when applying to marble.

• Mix one tablespoon clear household ammonia (3 percent solution) with a half cup water.

• Dampen a white rag in the solution and carefully rub the stain until it is gone. Then, rub the area with vinegar solution (see below) to avoid any skin irritation.

Vinegar

Used on glass, mirrors, laminates, and chrome, vinegar is an excellent disinfectant, cleaner, and hard-water stain remover.

• Mix one-third cup white vinegar with two-thirds cup water. Apply with a cloth.

DUSTING

When you dust, start at the top of the house and work your way down, remembering that dust falls and settles as you dislodge it. Do one room completely—seeing a newly dusted room will be a great incentive to move on to the next one.

Wood Furniture

• Quickly dust the tops of wooden tables at least every other day. Thoroughly dust once a week.

• For cleaning all wood furniture, choose a soft cotton rag—you can use your partner's old football jersey from his high-school days! Synthetic material won't absorb cleaning fluids; you need 100 percent cotton.

• The simplest way to dust is to wipe the surface using a cotton rag moistened—but not saturated—with plain water. However, this won't condition the wood in any way.

• Dust-removing sprays or cloths can be used on wooden surfaces, but avoid oils, which draw yet more dust and finger prints.

• Dust using a circular motion.

• Make sure you dust under table lamps and knickknacks.

• Dust intricate furnishings, such as those with carvings, with a small, soft brush, such as a natural-hair artist's brush or a dry, soft toothbrush.

• Clean all rags and brushes when you are finished.

• "Dusting mitts" pretreated with furniture polish are now on the market, which make the task even easier. Keep a box of them in your cleaning kit for ready access.

Glass-topped Tables and Monitor Screens

• Dust glass-topped tables and television screens twice a week with a soft rag and glass spray cleanser.

• Wipe down computer screens once a week. Check the manufacturer's or retailer's recommendations for special cleaning pads for optical plastic and glass.

Bibelots and Knickknacks

• Clean all objects twice a week.

• Dampen a soft rag with water and a few drops of nonabrasive detergent, and use to clean off your porcelain or china figurines.

• Clean crystal objects with a glass spray cleanser.

• Dry dust all books with a soft rag. Alternatively, use the upholstery nozzle of your vacuum cleaner.

USING A MOP

The following instructions are for wood floors and for everyday maintenance of tiled and stone floors.

• Mop your wood, tiled, and hard floors at least once a week. Heavily soiled areas, such as the entryway, kitchen, or bathroom, may need to be cleaned more frequently.

• Sweep the floor with a broom, an antistatic cloth mop, or a vacuum to remove as much dust as you can before you start mopping.

• Moisten your mop with clear water and an appropriate cleaner for the type of flooring. (Do not use soap on wood floors; instead, add a drop of wood-cleaning detergent to the water.)

• Rub the floor in a sweeping motion, forward and backward; do not use a circular motion.

• Lift the mop between strokes to avoid streaking the floor.

• Between strokes, shake off any dust that has gathered on the mop as you work. The mopping process will pick up any dust left behind by the broom.

• Use this mopping process for general, everyday maintenance of tile and stone floors in high-use areas.

• Choose a mop with a removable head that you can launder. String mops are best. Be sure to clean it regularly, and use bleach in the water to disinfect it.

USING A VACUUM CLEANER

• Keep carpets and rugs in top condition by regular vacuuming. Use doormats at the main entrances to your home to pick up soil from the street. Put casters under furniture to protect the carpets and rugs.

• Shampoo your carpets every one to two years, depending on whether you have young children and pets. If you have the latter, you may have to shampoo it more frequently, perhaps once every six months.

• Use the floor attachment on your vacuum cleaner for bare floors or valuable carpets or rugs.

• For regular carpeting, use a power-brush attachment.

• To maintain beautiful wood floors, vacuum them along the grain of the wood.

Which attachment to use?

Area to be vacuumed	Vacuum attachment
Cabinets, shelves, and books	all-purpose brush
Wood, stone, linoleum, or vinyl floors	floor brush
Narrow areas, detailing	radiator brush
Difficult places to clean	crevice nozzle
Baseboards and molding	dusting brush
Upholstery	upholstery nozzle

FLOORS

The essential character of a house is revealed in its floors. Whether they are hardwood, tile, stone, or laminate, your floors reflect the soul of your home and its fundamental design. A floor provides the depth and expanse to a room, and as such, it should be kept clean, uncluttered, and gleaming. Knowing how to clean all your floor surfaces is imperative for a well-kept home.

Granite and Stone

- Sweep up loose dirt every day with a dust mop, broom, or vacuum.
- Clean the floor on a weekly basis using a soft mop and water mixed with a small amount of neutral pH detergent. Don't use soap because it may leave a film.
- Wipe up spills immediately, as most stone is porous, so it stains easily.
- To remove grease or oil, use a commercial stain remover.
- Protect stone floors with a sealant once every three years.

Hardwood

- Sweep up loose dirt every day with a dust mop, broom, or vacuum.
- Vacuum thoroughly with a floor brush attachment once a week.
- Clean with a specialized wood floor cleaner. Use sudsy water on sealed wood.
- Do not apply furniture sprays or oils to the floor; they will make it slippery.

Linoleum

A resilient floor covering, linoleum stands up well to the wear suffered by a kitchen floor, making it a perfect choice for this room.

• Sweep up loose dirt every day with a dust mop, broom, or vacuum.
• Wash with soapy water and a sponge mop. Rinse with clear water and buff dry.
• You can wax with paste or liquid wax.

Tiles

Unglazed tiled floors don't show wear and tear like wood and marble, which (as long as a suitable treatment is applied) makes them good for kitchen floors.

• Sweep up loose dirt every day with a dust mop, broom, or vacuum.
• Wash once a week with a mild cleanser and a soft mop.

Vinyl

• Sweep up loose dirt every day. Vacuum thoroughly once a week.
• Mop the floor at least once a week with a neutral pH soap and warm water.
• Mopping vinyl regularly with a clean mop and mild detergent or floor cleaner will take care of most dirt and dust. If you want extra protection against germs, add a few drops of disinfectant to the water.
• Do not use abrasive cleansers.
• To remove scuff marks, use a nylon pad, sponge, or soft nylon brush dipped in an ammonia solution or isopropyl alcohol. Rinse well.

CARPETS

*To prolong the life of your carpets, vacuum them regularly.
Thorough vacuuming at least once a week, and more often in
heavy traffic areas, will remove dirt particles before they become
embedded in the pile. Shampoo your carpets from time to time.
For best results, get your carpet professionally cleaned.*

Spot Prevention

• To prevent dirt from the outside getting onto your carpet, put absorbent mats
at all the entrances to your home.

• Shake the mats outside and away from where people walk to prevent the dust
from being brought back in.

• Change filters in your heating and air-conditioning systems every six months to
prevent stains from forming around the vents.

• Clean high-traffic areas periodically with an absorbent powder.

• Do not apply stain-repellent treatments that contain silicone, because they tend
to accelerate carpet soiling.

Spot Removal Basics

• Act quickly whenever anything is dropped or spilled. Remove as much of the
spill as quickly as possible, using absorbent cloths or paper towels.

- Always work inward from the edge of the spill to prevent spreading it.
- Do not rub a spill, as it may cause the spot to spread or distort the pile.
- Blot up liquid spills with an absorbent white towel or thick paper towel. Pour soda water or seltzer sparingly over a liquid spill; the bubbles will cause more of the spilled substance to rise to the surface, which should then be blotted quickly.
- Scoop up solid spills with a spoon or the end of a knife.
- Once the spill is removed, most spots can be dealt with effectively, using the foam from the suds of a solution of water and a mild detergent. Otherwise, use the relevant spot-removal agent (see pages 34–35).
- For a wool carpet, or any wool blend, only use products which specify "Suitable for use on wool carpets."
- Never soak the carpet. After cleaning, blot as dry as possible with paper towels.
- Remove any remaining stain with carpet shampoo or commercial stain removers, following the product's instructions.
- Finally, rinse with clear, warm water, either by spraying the water onto the carpet, taking care not to get it too wet, or by patting it on with a clean white cloth or thick paper towel. Then blot dry thoroughly.
- Once dry, brush the pile back with the brush attachment of your vacuum cleaner.
- To raise the pile of a crushed carpet, cover the area with a damp cloth and hold a hot iron over the cloth. Brush up to lift the pile when the carpet is dry.

SPOT REMOVAL CHART FOR CARPETS

ITEM	STEP 1	STEP 2	STEP 3 (ORDER OF TREATMENT)
Alcoholic beverages	1	2	~
Bleach*	1	3	~
Blood	1	2	12
Butter	4	2	~
Candlewax	5	13	9
Chewing gum	5	4	~
Chocolate	2	3	6
Coffee	1	2	4
Colas and soft drinks	1	2	~
Cooking oils	4	2	~
Cream	2	4	~
Egg	4	2	~
Floor wax	4	2	~
Fruit juice	1	2	9

Cleaning agent

1. Sparkling water or cold tap water
2. Detergent solution or carpet-shampoo solution
3. Ammonia solution
4. Solvent
5. Chill with aerosol freezing agent or ice cubes in plastic bag. Pick or scrape off
6. Vinegar solution
7. Warm water
8. Clear nail-polish remover (preferably acetone)
9. Alcohol or mineral spirits, turpentine
10. Rust remover
11. Commercial absorbent cleaner
12. Professional cleaning
13. Absorbent paper and iron

ITEM	STEP 1	STEP 2	STEP 3 (ORDER OF TREATMENT)
Furniture polish	4	2	3
Gravy and sauces	7	2	~
Ink (fountain pen)	1	2	~
Ink (ballpoint)	4	9	2
Ink (felt tip)	7	2	8
Ketchup	7	2	~
Lipstick	4	2	~
Milk	7	4	2
Mustard	2	~	~
Nail polish	8	4	2
Oil and grease	4	2	~
Paint (latex)	1	2	4
Paint (oil)*	9	4	12
Rust	4	2	10
Salad dressing	2	4	~
Shoe polish	4	2	~
Soot	4	2	3
Tar	4	~	~
Tea	1	2	4
Urine (fresh)	1	2	~
Urine (old)	2	3	6
Vomit	2	~	~
Wine	1	2	~
Unknown material	4	11	2

* Unlikely to be removed

UPHOLSTERY

Regular vacuuming of upholstered furniture will help prevent soil accumulation. Do so once a week.

Spot Removal Basics

- Remove excess soil promptly by scraping off any residue with a dull knife or spoon, and/or blotting up spills with an absorbent cloth or paper towels.
- Be sure to pretest a cleaning solution in an inconspicuous spot before using it on the upholstery.
- Do not remove the cushion from its cover.
- Do not rub the spot; use a soft, white cloth or a clean sponge to apply the relevant cleaning solution.
- Rinse with a damp sponge, then dry immediately with a soft dry cloth.
- If the spot persists, call a professional upholstery cleaner.

Spot Removal Tips

Blood   Because blood coagulates, it must never be in contact with anything warm or hot. To clean, mix one teaspoon of very gentle detergent with one cup tepid water. Alternatively, mix one tablespoon ammonia with a half cup water. Apply either solution to the spot with a clean cloth, then tamp dry. Finally, sponge with clear water and tamp dry.

Chewing gum, ink Sponge with a small amount of drycleaning solvent. Alternatively, mix one teaspoon very gentle detergent with one cup tepid water. Apply to the spot with a clean cloth and tamp dry.

Chocolate, soil Mix one teaspoon very gentle detergent with one cup tepid water. Apply to the spot with a clean cloth and tamp dry. Then, mix one tablespoon ammonia with a half cup water. Apply to the spot with a clean cloth and tamp dry. Apply the detergent and water solution to the area again. Sponge with clear water and tamp dry.

Coffee, cola drinks Mix one teaspoon very gentle detergent with one cup tepid water. Apply to the spot with a clean cloth and tamp dry. Alternatively, mix one-third cup white vinegar with two-thirds cup tepid water. Apply to the spot with a clean cloth and tamp dry. Sponge with clear water and tamp dry.

Nail polish Daub with nail-polish remover (acetone) and tamp dry. Alternatively, mix one teaspoon very gentle detergent with one cup tepid water and blot with a clean cloth. Sponge with clear water and tamp dry.

Soft drinks (other than cola), wine Mix one teaspoon very gentle detergent with one cup tepid water. Apply to the spot with a clean cloth and tamp dry. Then mix one-third cup white vinegar with two-thirds cup water. Apply to the spot with a clean cloth and tamp dry. If necessary, repeat the first step.

THE HEART OF THE HOME

GLEAMING KITCHENS

Your kitchen is the heart of your home, where your family's food is prepared, stored, mixed, and measured. Make it a special place, suited to your convenience, so you always know where to find what you need. Keep fresh food on hand; chopping blocks, pots, pans, and countertops, meticulously cleaned; and you can look forward to donning your apron and whipping up a delicious feast with ease whenever you like.

THE DAILY ROUTINE

If time is short, the kitchen is the one room that should be kept clean over and above the others. Food scraps, dirt, and grime must be dealt with so the hub of the home is kept clean and germ-free. Establish a definite routine based on your needs and those of your family, so your kitchen remains neat, as well as stress-free, around mealtimes. It is fun to bake cookies with your five-year-old ... but only if you've organized yourself ahead of time so you can stay one step ahead of your baby Escoffier!

Kitchen Basics

• Begin your day with spotlessly clean utensils and washed-down countertops.

• Change dishtowels daily, or as necessary.

• Glasses, dishes, and sharp knives should be put away after use to avoid breakages and nasty accidents.

• Take a quick look in your refrigerator to check what you will need for meals that day or week. Keep an on-going list of fresh food and pantry items you require, so you have a complete list for the next time you do your weekly shopping.

• Store all kitchen cleaning products in their caddy within easy reach of appliances. An ideal place for them is under the kitchen sink, although if you have young children, make sure the cupboard has secure child locks. It may be better to store all cleaning products and other chemicals out of reach if the family is young.

• Clean up after every meal; wash countertops with a cloth dampened with warm sudsy water or disinfectant kitchen spray for tougher food spills.

• Wipe down the oven door and top of the cooktop after every use. This can be done with a cloth or paper towel dampened with a commercial window cleaner.

• Empty trashcans and liners and reline the cans at the end of every day. Keep a supply of folded plastic trash bags at the bottom of the can before relining, so they will be right there for use when you need them.

• When preparing meals, keep a small receptacle handy for discarding cooking refuse, such as trimmed fat, asparagus stalks, chicken bones, and so on.

KITCHEN APPLIANCES

The kitchen remains the central part of the home. Appliances vary from house to house, depending on individual needs. The latest kitchen appliances are convenient and easy to use, and help us in our everyday tasks, but to get the best use out of them they must be cleaned regularly. Make it a habit to wipe down exterior surfaces of all appliances after each use and sanitize the interiors regularly, according to the manufacturer's instructions.

REFRIGERATOR
Your refrigerator needs to be kept rigorously clean and hygienic. Here are the basic recommendations for upkeep.

Daily
- Check all fresh food items for spoilage and throw out anything that has spoiled.
- Check expiration dates on cheese, eggs, and milk; discard what has expired.
- Wipe up liquid spills or food particles with a scrupulously clean, damp cloth— not the one used to clean the counter or floor!
- Make sure that all leftover foods are stored in airtight glass or plastic containers.
- Wipe the door handle. For stubborn stains, use a disinfectant spray or a baking-soda paste made from two parts baking soda and one part water.

Weekly

• Clean the inside of the refrigerator with a sponge and hot, soapy water.

• Remove the shelves and wash them in the sink with hot water and detergent. Rinse well and dry.

• Wipe the door compartments and insides of the refrigerator with a solution made from two tablespoons baking soda and one quart warm water. Rinse and dry.

• Wash the door seal with warm water and a mild detergent. Rinse and dry. Apply petroleum jelly to the seal occasionally.

• Remove the produce drawers and wash them in the sink with warm water and a mild detergent.

• Wash the freezer compartment with a solution made from two tablespoons baking soda and one quart warm water. Rinse and dry.

Monthly

• Vacuum the condenser coils at the back of the refrigerator if they are exposed.

• Defrost the freezer every two to three months. Some freezers today are self-defrosting; but if you don't have one that is, you will need to defrost your freezer manually. To do so, first empty the freezer and turn it off. Put bowls of boiling water inside, and as it defrosts, wipe out the water and residue with a clean cloth.

COOKTOPS AND GRIDDLES

Used most days if you cook regularly at home, burners soon get grimy from use, accumulating spills, oils, and fats. Wipe up spills immediately and wipe down the area daily with a damp cloth. This will keep it hygienic, and prevent fires or accidents.

Cooktops and Burner Grates

Cooktops are made of baked-on enamel, stainless steel, or black glass.

- Wait until the stove is cool before you clean it.
- Remove drip pans and soak in hot, sudsy water.
- Spray the surface of the cooktop with an all-purpose cleanser or a solution made from one part vinegar to one part water.
- Wipe with a sponge or clean cloth. Wipe excess with a paper towel.
- Use a baking-soda paste on tough spots. Wipe down with a damp sponge.
- Scour pans with a nylon-type non-scratching pad, if necessary. Dry with a thick paper towel.

Hobs

Hobs are usually made of hard, heavy-duty plastic or synthetic material.

- Hobs can be taken off and immersed in a bowl of hot, sudsy water.
- For tougher-to-clean caked-on oil and scum, use an old toothbrush soaked in liquid scouring cleanser and water.

Glass Sealed Range Tops

- Wait until the stove is cool.
- Spray with a general-purpose cleanser or clean with a solution made from one part vinegar to one part water.
- Wipe with a sponge or clean cloth.
- Apply a baking soda paste, scrub gently, and rinse.

Gas Griddles

- The cast aluminum griddle has a non-stick coating for easy cleaning. For best results, the manufacturer recommends that you wash the surface with hot, soapy water, rinse, and dry.
- Do not use steel wool or coarse scouring pads or powders.
- The nonstick surface requires periodic conditioning to preserve the easy-release quality of the surface. Condition the nonstick surface by brushing with cooking oil and wipe off any excess.
- When cooking, don't use metal cooking utensils, which have a tendency to scratch the nonstick coating. Use plastic, wooden, or bamboo utensils.

OVENS

Clean your oven once a week if you cook every day, and every two weeks if you cook less frequently. Having a spanking-clean oven keeps your kitchen sweet-smelling, and prevents your food from smelling of yesterday's leftovers.

Outside of the Oven

• For stainless-steel panels, use a specialized stainless-steel cleanser. Remove finger marks with a soft cloth and a few drops of baby oil or rinse aid.

• For glass panels, spray with window cleaner or a multisurface kitchen cleaner.

• Soak grates, knobs, and drip pans in hot, soapy water. Use a stiff brush to remove any burned-on grease.

Self-cleaning Ovens

• Always refer to the oven's manual, which describes in detail how to turn on the self-cleaning mechanism.

• Most standard ovens take approximately four hours to be thoroughly cleaned.

• A quick wipe with a dry cloth after the self-cleaning process is all that's needed.

Cleaning Ovens Manually

• Your oven should be cleaned according to the type of linings or cleaning systems it has. Refer to the oven's manual for specific directions.

- Always wear rubber gloves and make sure the kitchen is well ventilated.
- To remove baked-on food remnants, first pry off what you can with a dull knife.
- For normal oven maintenance, use hot, soapy water.
- For easy-to-clean areas, use regular detergent or a liquid cleanser.
- Spray stubborn remaining spots with a commercial or homemade oven cleaner (see below) and use a scouring pad.
- If you don't have time to clean the oven during the day, you can leave the oven to clean overnight. First, loosen grime with a dull knife. Warm the oven then turn it off. Put a small bowl of ammonia on the top rack of the still-warm oven and a pan of water on the lower rack. Make sure the oven is inaccessible to children or pets. Leave overnight. In the morning, open the kitchen windows for ventilation, then wipe out the oven with thick paper towels.

Homemade Oven Cleaner

This oven cleaner is for use on untreated enamel linings only. Do not use on self-cleaning or nonstick ovens.

- Wet the inside surfaces of the oven and sprinkle with baking soda.
- Rub with a steel wool pad, then wipe off the grime with a soft cloth.
- Repeat the process, if necessary.
- Rinse well and dry.
- Save the commercial oven cleaner for the burned-on mess. It is more caustic.

KITCHEN DRAINS

If you follow the advice given below, you will help to keep your drains clean and clear, prevent clogs and unsanitary conditions, and also help to avoid any unpleasant smells from developing.

Avoiding Clogged-up Drains

• Purchase a drain strainer. This fits over the plughole, allowing water to drain through it, but catches any food particles that get into the sink. They are available from hardware stores.

• Grease and oil cause clogging. Be sure never to pour leftover fat down the drain. Instead, pour it into a can or jar, cover well, and refrigerate—then throw it out.

• While you are cooking, keep a very small trash container for food debris close by. Any kitchen store should have a mini size. Line it with the smallest trashcan liner available and use it for discarding cooking scraps. Likewise, when rinsing your plates and dishes after a meal, make sure you put as many of the leftovers as possible into the mini trashcan to keep food debris from getting into the drain. After you have finished preparing and eating your meal, remove the liner from the mini trashcan and discard it, and replace it with a new one.

• To prevent a buildup of grease in the sink and waste pipes, flush them once a week with a solution made from one cup washing soda crystals and two-and-a-half cups hot water. Alternatively, use a commercial drain cleanser.

Homemade Cleansers for Regular Maintenance

To *clean and deodorize* Pour three-quarters cup baking soda down the drain, and then slowly drip warm water into it. Alternatively, mix three-quarters cup washing soda in one gallon warm water. First, pour hot water down the drain, then pour down the baking soda solution, followed by more hot water. Use either method once every two weeks to keep the drain clear.

To *disinfect and sanitize* Add just less than one cup chlorine bleach and one tablespoon powdered laundry detergent to one gallon warm water. Pour the solution into the sink, let it drain, then rinse with warm water. Do this once a month.

Homemade Cleansers for Clogged Drains

• Pour a half cup baking soda down the drain, followed by one cup vinegar. Alternatively, mix two teaspoons ammonia with one quart boiling water and pour down the drain. Use a plunger after either solution.

• Eco-friendly enzymatic drain openers can be put down the drain. These are freeze-dried blocks of bacillus bacteria, which eat the material clogging the drain.

BATHROOM BLISS

BEAUTIFUL BATHROOMS

The measure of a well-kept home can be found in its bathrooms, which should be spotless, germ-free, shiny, and sweet-smelling. Keeping your family healthy begins by maintaining a well-supplied bathroom, which is devoid of mildew, soap scum, and mineral stains. This room can also become your sacred space—a place to which you can retreat to relax. Make it your haven by filling it with specially chosen products, towels, and scents.

THE DAILY ROUTINE

It doesn't take much time to keep your bathroom spotless and glowing. For general maintenance, just a few minutes every day will usually suffice. Wipe the shower and sink(s) after each use if you have time. Keep cleaning products tucked away in their caddy inside a cabinet for a quick sanitizing of the toilet.

Bathroom Basics

• Frequency of cleaning should not vary.

• Use separate cleaning cloths, tools, or sponges for those areas of the bathroom with high populations of germs and bacteria—the toilet, toilet lid, and floor or cabinet walls near the toilet. As a general rule, move from low contamination areas to high ones.

• Frequently used toilets should be cleaned every day. Use a clean rag and a spray disinfectant to wipe down the rim of the bowl and seat. Use a brush and a standard toilet-bowl liquid or gel cleanser for the toilet bowl. Gels are better because they stay in contact with the bowl for longer.

• Bathtubs that are used frequently should be wiped down daily.

• Invest in a "catch-all" for your shower drain—a plastic strainer that goes over the drain to catch hair as you shower. This will prevent the drain from getting blocked.

• Keep a plastic squeegee in the shower to wipe off the glass and tiles immediately after showering to prevent nasty water spots from appearing. If the squeegee is on hand, you won't need to search for it.

• Keep a clean, soft rag or sponge available to wipe off the sinks and countertops, but don't ever use the same one on or around the toilet.

• Store a dry cloth in an undercounter caddy to polish any chrome fixtures after use. If you wipe them immediately, you will prevent water spotting, which is more difficult to remove if left to air dry.

• Keep a mirror cleaner and a disinfectant spray handy.

• In order to maintain good air quality, it is essential to ventilate your bathroom as soon as it has been used. Opening the windows after you shower is the best form of ventilation. It's also a good idea to invest in a good fan system in the toilet area. Air fresheners are effective, too, but nothing beats fresh air.

FIXTURES AND FITTINGS

Your bathroom fixtures need to be kept meticulously clean. A bathroom caddy holding all the necessary cleaning products and tools will make this task easier. A freshly scrubbed bathroom is not only inviting, it can become your haven after a hard day.

TOILETS

Okay, so it's not the nicest job in the world, but it's easy to do if you have a toilet-bowl brush and caddy stored next to the toilet. There are many good toilet cleaners to choose from; always keep one close by for a quick sanitizing of the toilet on a daily basis.

Routine Maintenance

- Clean outside the toilet bowl with a disinfectant cleanser.
- Toilet-bowl cleansers of all sorts will not harm vitreous china toilets.
- Sprinkle a powdered cleanser into the toilet and scrub with a stiff nylon brush.
- For stubborn spots, use a soft nylon-bristle brush and undiluted liquid detergent.
- In hard-water areas, use a combined cleaner and mineral remover.
- Never leave products on for too long; otherwise, the chemicals could penetrate the surface through worn areas or cracks in the glaze, resulting in discoloration.
- To prevent clogs, pour one cup baking soda into the toilet once a week, then flush.

Disinfecting the Toilet Bowl

• Toilet-bowl cleaners should be used daily, or at least once a week.
• Use a long-handled rim brush to clean the rim holes and to clean as far into the trap as possible to prevent mineral deposits from forming. Alternatively, use a mousse that expands under the rim.
• A toilet block under the rim will keep it smelling fresh and protect against germs.
• Add disinfectant to the toilet bowl and leave for 30 minutes.
• Clean the toilet brush by swirling it around the toilet bowl, then let it stand in a fresh mixture of disinfectant in the toilet bowl for 20 minutes.
• While the brush is soaking, wash the toilet brush stand with disinfectant cleanser.
• Rinse the brush and replace it in the stand.

Mineral Deposit Removal

• Daily use of a standard toilet-bowl cleanser with built-in mineral-deposit protection should be enough to keep deposits at bay. If not, use a commercial remover for bathroom fixtures or a bleach solution, and scrub with a long-handled brush.
• In hard-water areas, keep the holes in the rim clear for proper bowl flushing.
• Homemade mineral-deposit remover: Soak a rag or paper towel in white vinegar and leave it on the trouble spot for one hour. This is effective in softening the mineral deposit for easier removal.

BATHTUBS AND BASINS

There are many styles and types of tubs and sinks from which to choose, such as porcelain, enamel, fiberglass, and acrylic. Nothing looks more inviting than a freshly scrubbed sink or tub. Generally, a quick wipe after use will suffice to remove scum, but there are also wonderful spray-on sink and tub cleaners widely available.

Porcelain Enamel Tubs and Sinks

• Wash with a gentle, all-purpose cleanser.
• Remove hard-water stains with a solution of one part white vinegar and one part water, or use a commercial deposit remover for bathroom fixtures. Rinse thoroughly and dry with a clean rag.

Fiberglass and Acrylic Tubs

• Follow the manufacturer's instructions. If they are not readily available, call any good plumbing supply store for how best to clean.
• For stubborn stains, use a nylon bristle brush and undiluted dishwashing liquid. Never use abrasive cleansers.

Stainless Steel Sinks

• Make a cleaning solution from four tablespoons baking soda dissolved in one quart water. Wipe around the sink, using a cloth dipped in this solution. Wipe dry with a clean cloth, and polish with a dry cloth.

• Alternatively, clean with a powdered all-purpose cleanser and a soft sponge, as necessary, depending on usage.

• Rub lightly with the grain when cleaning.

• For tough streaks and water spots, remove with a cloth dampened with isopropyl alcohol, then let air dry.

• Do not use bleach on stainless steel.

FAUCETS AND SHOWERSETS

As the "jewels" of your bathroom, your fixtures should shine. Always wipe faucets and shower sets after use to prevent water spots or stains. Faucets usually come in chrome, which is a plate finish for brass metal. Simple maintenance includes wiping off with a dry cloth after use, and occasional washing with a gentle cleanser. Do not use metal polishes, spray polishes, or acidic cleansers.

Polished Chrome

• Clean with mild soap and water, using a soft sponge; then dry with a soft, clean cloth.

• Do not use abrasive cleansers. To clean stubborn spots, use undiluted liquid detergent or a nonabrasive commercial bathroom cleanser.

• Cleaning frequency depends on usage. Weekly applications give best results.

• After polishing, apply a paste wax to add another temporary protective coat.

• To keep shower fixtures beautiful, always dry them after use. After you've wiped the wet tiles, use a clean, dry rag to polish the fixtures. This should be done after each use to prevent water spots.

• Remove rust or hard-water deposits with any mildly acidic solution, such as a mixture of one part white vinegar or lemon juice and one part water, or a commercial mineral-deposit remover.

Plastic

• If your showerhead is made of plastic and there is mineral buildup on it, remove the head and soak it in a mixture of one part vinegar and one part water for a few hours. Don't soak polished nickel in a vinegar/water mixture, or it will tarnish; use a commercial product instead. Check instructions first.

SHOWER ENCLOSURES
This small space traps moisture and unwanted soap buildup. To prevent scum, wipe showers after each use and clean thoroughly every week.

Routine Maintenance

• Wipe off and rinse the shower stall after every use.
• Remove grime and soap scum as necessary with water and a soft rag. Do not use any chemicals or abrasive cleansers. If water spots persist after using water and a soft rag, try a small amount of commercial bathroom cleanser or shower spray.
• Counters and walls in shower stalls and those near tubs and sinks need to be cleaned once a week with an all-purpose cleanser to prevent a buildup of scum.
• Spray tiles and shower curtain (if plastic) with a bathroom cleanser. Wipe off, then rinse. Tamp dry.
• To remove mildew from shower curtains, scrub with a bleach solution and rinse thoroughly.

INDEX

PHOTOGRAPHY CREDITS BY PAGE

Debi Treloar endpapers, 1, 2, 8–9, 10 left, 10 right, 23 left, 30–31; Chris Everard 38–39, 40 left, 54 left, 54 right, 57, 58, 61, 62; James Merrell 3, 20–21, 40 right, 41, 42, 51; David Montgomery 24, 52–53, 55; Andrew Wood 4, 19, 33; Jan Baldwin 6, 27, 36; Caroline Arber 23 right; Christopher Drake 46; Dan Duchars 15; Simon Upton 16

LOCATION CREDITS

4 designed by Littman Goddard Hogarth Architects (+44 (0)20 7351 7871/www.lgh-architects.co.uk); 6 the Meiré family home, designed by Marc Meiré (meirefamily@aol.com); 8–9 Mark and Sally of Baileys Home and Garden's house in Herefordshire (+44 (0)1989 563015/ www.baileyshomeandgarden.com); 10 left Debi Treloar's family home in north-west London; 10 right Catherine Chermayeff & Jonathan David's family home in New York, designed by Asfour Guzy Architects (212-334-9350/easfour@asfourguzy.com); 38–39 Kampfner's house in London designed by Ash Sakula Architects (+44 (0)20 7837 9735/ www.ashsak.com); 40 left Peter and Nicole Dawes' apartment, designed by Mullman Seidman Architects (212-431-0770/ www.mullmanseidman.com); 54 left designed by John Minshaw, London (+44 (0)20 7258 5777/ enquiries@johnminshawdesigns.com); 54 right designed by Orefelt Associates, London (+44 (0)20 7243 3181/orefelt@msn.com); 57 designed by Gabellini Associates, New York (212-388-1700/www.gabelliniassociates.com); 61 designed by Bruno Tanquerel, Paris (+33 1 43 57 03 93)